CYBER BOSS
CONSULTING

CYBERSECURITY CAREER BLUEPRINT:

FAST-TRACKING YOUR WAY TO SUCCESS

DANIELLE ROBINSON

Disclaimer

The information in this book is provided for educational and informational purposes only. References to companies, products, services, tools, and organizations (including but not limited to Deloitte, Intel, CGI, Microsoft, CrowdStrike, and others) are made solely for descriptive or illustrative purposes. All trademarks, logos, and brand names are the property of their respective owners.

The inclusion of these names does not imply any affiliation, sponsorship, endorsement, or partnership between the author, Cyber Boss Consulting, and the referenced entities. Any mention of individuals' employment at these companies reflects factual information at the time of writing and is subject to change.

While every effort has been made to ensure the accuracy and timeliness of the information, the author and publisher make no representations or warranties regarding completeness, reliability, or future applicability. The field of cybersecurity is constantly evolving, and practices, technologies, and industry standards may change after publication.

The author and publisher disclaim any liability for losses, damages, or claims arising from the use or misuse of the information contained in this book. Readers are encouraged to verify current details independently and seek professional advice when necessary.

CONTENTS

PART 1

UNDERSTANDING THE CYBERSECURITY LANDSCAPE

INTRODUCTION:

WHY CYBERSECURITY, WHY NOW

If you're reading this, you're probably not looking for "just a job." You want something better. Something challenging. Something that pays the bills and still leaves you feeling like you're doing work that matters. Well, welcome to cybersecurity. It's exciting, it's growing like crazy, and yes... it's full of drama. The bad guys are getting smarter, the attacks are getting nastier, and the good guys? We're still trying to catch up. That's where you come in.

The Exploding Demand for Cybersecurity Professionals

Here's the reality. There are hundreds of thousands of open cybersecurity jobs in the U.S. right now and millions across the globe. Every type of organization is desperate for help — hospitals, banks, tech companies, even mom-and-pop shops that have finally realized "cyber" isn't just for big corporations. Criminals are organized, well-funded, and have all day to find ways to break in. We don't. Which means we need more smart people in this fight... yesterday.

How Your Background Gives You an Edge

Whether you're a student, a veteran, or an IT pro, you're already ahead of the game. Students? You bring fresh ideas and zero bad habits from years of corporate nonsense. Veterans? You've got discipline, problem-solving skills, and the ability to function under pressure (also, you know how to follow orders... which managers love). IT pros? You already understand networks, systems, and why "turn it off and back on again" sometimes works. You've got transferable skills. Now it's just about learning how to speak the language of cybersecurity.

Why the Industry Needs You

Cyberattacks aren't slowing down. They're getting faster, nastier, and more expensive. Hospitals are being locked out of their own systems. Data breaches are costing companies millions. State-sponsored hackers are doing everything from stealing research to trying to mess with power grids. And here's the kicker...there just aren't enough skilled people to stop them. This isn't just a good career move. It's an open invitation to step up and make a real difference.

The Truth About Breaking In

Let's clear this up right now. There's no magic course, no 30-day bootcamp, no "become a hacker overnight" trick that will drop a six-figure job in your lap. If someone's selling you that dream, they're also probably selling "get rich quick" real estate seminars at a Holiday Inn conference room. But here's the good news, there is a clear, proven path to get into this field. It's not about being a genius. It's about learning the right skills, getting real experience, and knowing how to show employers you can do the job.

Why The Lab @ Cyber Boss Consulting Exists

The biggest problem for beginners is the gap between "I learned this in a class" and "I can actually do this on the job." Employers want proof. They want to know if you've touched the tools, handled incidents, and solved problems in real time. That's why I created The Lab. It's a hands-on, real-world training program where you work with the same tools Fortune 500 companies use. Microsoft Sentinel, Defender, CrowdStrike, and you're guided by people who do this work every day. The Lab's instructors include cybersecurity professionals whose experience spans Fortune 500 companies such as Deloitte, Accenture, Intel, and CGI (note: these companies are not affiliated with or endorsing The Lab). By the end, you don't just have knowledge... you have stories, projects, and experience you can put on your resume. And in cybersecurity, that's gold.

So here we are. The jobs are open. The need is real. And you've got every reason to make your move. Let's get started before the bad guys get any further ahead.

CHAPTER 1:

WHAT CYBERSECURITY REALLY IS (AND ISN'T)

When most people hear "cybersecurity," they picture the same thing. A hoodie-wearing hacker hunched over a laptop in a dark room, green code running down the screen like a scene from The Matrix. Let's burst that bubble right now.

That is not real life.

In the real world, cybersecurity is a massive, layered field that involves engineers, analysts, policymakers, project managers, compliance pros, and yes, a few people who still wear hoodies, but usually because the server room is freezing.

It is not all "hacking." Most cybersecurity professionals will spend years without doing anything that looks like the movies. Instead, they are monitoring systems, setting up defenses, investigating incidents, training staff, and making sure the company stays on the right side of the law when it collects your data.

If that sounds less Hollywood and more like an actual job, good. You are already ahead of most people who apply for cyber roles.

Busting the Myths

Let's clear up a few things right now.

Myth 1: You must be a genius coder to work in cybersecurity. Not true. Coding helps in some roles, but plenty of cyber pros can barely write a "Hello World" script. Many jobs focus on analysis, compliance, policy, or configuring tools, not coding.

Myth 2: Cybersecurity is all about catching hackers. Sorry, CSI: Cyber lied to you. We spend more time preventing attacks and keeping systems secure than we do chasing bad guys in dramatic foot chases. Although that would make staff meetings more interesting.

Myth 3: You need ten years of experience to get your first cyber job. Nope. What you need is the right mix of knowledge, practical skills, and the ability to prove you can do the work.

Myth 4: It is a "tech-only" field. Also, not true. There is plenty of room for people who can write policies, train employees, manage risks, and translate tech talk into plain English for executives.

The Core Areas of Cybersecurity

Cybersecurity is not one thing. It is a collection of specialties that work together. Here are some of the main ones:

- Security Engineering – The Builders. They design and set up security tools, firewalls, and systems that protect networks. If you like problem-solving and tinkering with technology, this could be your lane.

- Governance, Risk, and Compliance (GRC) – The rule keepers. They make sure the company follows laws, regulations, and best practices. This is great for people who are detail-oriented and love spotting loopholes.

- Security Operations Center (SOC) – The front line. SOC analysts watch alerts, investigate suspicious activity, and respond to incidents in real time. If you like action, this is where it happens.

- Penetration Testing (Ethical Hacking) – The breakers. They try to hack systems legally to find weaknesses before the bad guys do. Perfect for curious minds who like to push limits.

- Cloud Security – The cloud protectors. As more companies move to AWS, Azure, or Google Cloud, these specialists make sure data in the cloud stays safe. Great for those who enjoy working with modern tech.

- Incident Response – The firefighters of the cyber world. When something goes wrong, they figure out what happened, contain the damage, and make sure it does not happen again. Best for people who stay calm under pressure.

Finding the Role That Fits You

The beauty of cybersecurity is that there is a place for almost every personality type.

If you love fast-paced problem-solving, SOC or Incident Response might be your thing. If you prefer careful, methodical work, GRC or Security Engineering could be a better fit. If you like thinking like the bad guy to stop the bad guy, pen testing is your playground. If you want to mix technology with strategy, Cloud Security or Security Architecture could be perfect.

Cybersecurity is not about fitting into one mold. It is about finding where your strengths meet the industry's needs and building from there.

So, forget the hoodie stereotype. This is a team sport. We need strategists, builders, investigators, communicators, and yes, the occasional hacker. The question is not whether there is a place for you. The question is whether you are ready to claim it.

CHAPTER 2:

THE SKILLS THAT MATTER MOST

Here is the truth. Getting into cybersecurity is not about memorizing a giant list of buzzwords or sprinkling random tech terms into conversations. It is about having the skills employers care about and being able to prove you can use them.

And yes, those skills are more than just the "technical" stuff. You can be the most brilliant network engineer in the world, but if you cannot explain your findings to a manager without making their eyes glaze over, you will not get very far.

Let's break it down.

The Technical Skills Employers Want

You do not need to master every tool and technology before applying for a job, but you do need a solid foundation. Think of these as your core building blocks.

Networking Fundamentals: Understand how devices talk to each other, how data moves through a network, and what "normal" traffic looks like so you can spot trouble. Learn IP addresses, subnets, ports, and protocols. If you can explain what a firewall does to your grandma without confusing her, you are on the right track.

Cloud Fundamentals: More companies are moving to AWS, Azure, and Google Cloud, which means you need to know how cloud environments work and how to secure them. You do not have to be a cloud architect, but you should understand cloud storage, access controls, and basic cloud security.

SIEM Tools: Security Information and Event Management systems like Microsoft Sentinel, Splunk, or QRadar collect logs and alerts from across a network. Hands-on experience with these tools shows you can detect and respond to threats which employers love.

Scripting and Automation: You do not need to be a full-time programmer, but knowing some Python, PowerShell, or Bash can help you automate repetitive tasks, analyze data faster, and generally look like a wizard to your team.

The Soft Skills That Make You Stand Out

Technical skills might get you noticed. Soft skills will keep you in the game.

Problem-Solving: Cybersecurity is a puzzle that is always changing. You must be curious, creative, and relentless in finding solutions.

Communication: At some point, you will have to explain a security issue to someone who thinks "malware" is a computer virus that can be cured with chicken soup. If you can translate technical problems into plain language, you will be an asset.

Teamwork: You will work with IT, developers, compliance officers, executives, and maybe even law enforcement. You cannot be the "I work alone" type if you want to succeed.

Transferable Skills You Might Already Have

One of the best things about cybersecurity is that you do not have to start from scratch. Many skills from other careers fit perfectly into this field.

From the Military: Veterans bring discipline, mission focus, adaptability, and the ability to perform under pressure. Those skills are invaluable in incident response, SOC roles, and leadership positions.

From IT: If you have been in IT, you already understand networks, systems, troubleshooting, and maybe even security configurations. That experience transitions naturally into cyber engineering, cloud security, or SOC work.

From Law Enforcement and Investigations: Law enforcement officers and investigators know how to gather evidence, follow chain-of-custody rules, interview witnesses, and piece together the "who, what, when, where, and why" of an incident. Those skills are gold in digital forensics, insider threat programs, and incident response.

From Compliance and Regulatory Roles: If you have worked in compliance, auditing, or regulatory affairs, you understand the importance of rules, documentation, and risk management. This experience transfers perfectly into GRC (Governance, Risk, and Compliance) roles in cybersecurity.

From Healthcare: Healthcare professionals deal with privacy, compliance (think HIPAA), and protecting sensitive data every day. You also know how to work in high-stress, high-stakes environments where mistakes have serious consequences, a perfect match for roles that require attention to detail and patient data security.

From Academia or Other Professions: Teachers, researchers, analysts, and even people from unrelated fields bring valuable skills like data analysis, project management, clear writing, training, and public speaking. These are critical for cybersecurity awareness programs, policy creation, and technical documentation.

Cybersecurity is not just about tech. It is about people who can solve problems, adapt quickly, and understand both the technical and human sides of security. You might already have more of what it takes than you realize. The next step is figuring out where those skills fit and how to position yourself for the role you want.

And that is exactly what we will dive into in the next chapter.

CHAPTER 3

MAPPING THE CAREER PATHS

By now you are probably wondering what the actual job options look like in cybersecurity. And if you have done any Googling, you have probably been told you can waltz right into a six-figure "entry-level" position with no experience if you can pass a multiple-choice certification exam.

Yeah... no.

Let's be real. There are entry-level titles and then there are realistic first jobs. They are not always the same thing, and knowing the difference can save you a lot of frustration.

Entry-Level Roles vs. Realistic First Roles

The internet is full of lists like "Top 10 Entry Level Cybersecurity Jobs," and sure, the titles sound amazing. Cybersecurity Analyst. Penetration Tester. Incident Responder. Cloud Security Engineer. They make it sound like you are going to be running the show on day one.

In reality, most people start with roles that are a step toward those big titles rather than the big titles themselves. And that is okay.

A true entry-level job in cyber is one where the employer knows you will need some training and guidance. These are often found in Security Operations Centers (SOC Analyst Tier 1), junior compliance roles, IT support positions with security responsibilities, or assistant roles in risk management or governance.

A realistic first job might also be one that is not even labeled "cybersecurity" but still gives you security exposure. Think IT Help Desk where you manage account permissions and troubleshoot endpoint protection issues. Or a systems administrator role where you handle patching and backups. Or a compliance coordinator job where you work with HIPAA or PCI-DSS requirements.

The point is, do not get so hung up on job titles that you miss the stepping stones that get you in the game.

The Get In, Level Up, Specialize Strategy

Here is a career strategy that works for most people:

Step One – Get In: Take the role that gets your foot in the door. It might not be your dream job. You might even feel like it is "beneath" you based on your other experience. Take it anyway if it moves you closer to a security-focused position.

Step Two – Level Up: Once you are in, you start collecting wins. You learn the tools your team uses. You get additional certifications that make sense for your role. You take on projects that stretch your skills. You volunteer for security-related work even if it is not in your job description. The goal is to build a portfolio of experience that screams "I am ready for more."

Step Three – Specialize: After you have built a solid foundation, you pick a lane. Maybe you will become a SOC expert, a cloud security specialist, a GRC pro, or a penetration tester. This is where you start to stand out because you have depth in one area while still understanding the big picture. Specialists are where the money and job security really live.

Salary Expectations and Growth Opportunities

Let's talk money, because let's be honest, part of why you are here is the paycheck.

In the United States, realistic starting salaries for entry-level cyber roles are often in the $55,000 to $75,000 range depending on location, industry, and your background. If you already have IT, military, or related experience, you can push toward the higher end.

Once you move into more specialized or senior roles, salaries climb quickly. Mid-level positions can land you between $85,000 and $120,000. Senior roles and niche specialties like penetration testing, cloud security architecture, and incident response can easily hit $130,000 to $160,000 or more.

And then there are leadership positions. If you climb the ladder to become a CISO (Chief Information Security Officer) or Director of Security, you are looking at $180,000 to $250,000 plus bonuses in many markets. And yes, that comes with 24/7 responsibility and a stress level that could probably power a small city.

The good news is that cybersecurity has one of the clearest upward growth paths of any career. Every skill you add and every problem you solve makes you more valuable.

Cybersecurity careers are not about jumping straight into the deep end. They are about finding the smartest entry point, building a solid foundation, and then climbing like your future depends on it. Because it does. And if you do it right, you will look back and realize that first "meh" job was exactly what you needed to get to where you really wanted to be.

PART 2:

PREPARING FOR THE TRANSITION

CHAPTER 4:

ASSESSING WHERE YOU ARE NOW

Before you can figure out how to get where you want to go in cybersecurity, you have to know exactly where you are starting from. Most people skip this part because it feels boring compared to browsing cool job titles or daydreaming about that "future six-figure salary."

But here is the thing. If you do not know your current skills and gaps, you will waste time chasing roles you are not ready for or paying for training you do not even need.

Think of this as planning a road trip. You cannot just say, "I am going to California" without knowing whether you are starting in Nevada or New York. Your path, speed, and stops along the way all depend on where you are right now.

Step One –Take a Skills Inventory

Make a list of every skill you have that could apply to cybersecurity. Include technical skills like networking, cloud, scripting, or using SIEM tools. Do not forget soft skills like problem solving, communication, and teamwork.

Be brutally honest. This is not the time to claim "cloud security experience" because you once saved a photo to Google Drive. Rate each skill as beginner, intermediate, or advanced based on what you can do right now, not what you think you might figure out after watching a few YouTube tutorials.

Step Two – Identify the Gaps

Once you know what you have, compare it to what employers are asking for in the roles you want. Those missing pieces are your gaps. They are not failures. They are just your personal to-do list for breaking into the field.

Step Three – Let AI Help You Figure It Out

You do not have to figure this out alone. AI tools like ChatGPT can speed up your self-assessment and give you a clearer picture of where you stand.

Thinking about getting into cybersecurity but don't know where to start?

Upload your resume and let ChatGPT do the heavy lifting.

Here's a prompt you can copy and paste:

> "Act as an expert career consultant with 30 years of experience helping people transition into different industries. I want to transition into Cybersecurity. I am not sure what I want to do exactly. Based on my resume, give me a list of (X) jobs I would be a good fit for and why. Tell me how they align with my goals and who I am. Also, please give me a comprehensive, step-by-step plan to attain each job title. Ask me questions, one at a time, for the information you need."

🔥 Pro Tip: Upload your most recent resume directly into ChatGPT. Make sure it includes:

✅ Your certifications
✅ Transferable skills
✅ Work history
✅ Accomplishments
✅ Special projects
✅ Training and internships
✅ Education

This one exercise can give you clarity on what roles match your background and exactly what you need to learn next. It is like having a career coach in your back pocket.

Step Four – Translate Your Experience into Cybersecurity Language

Your resume might not scream "cybersecurity" yet, but that does not mean your experience is not valuable. You just need to connect the dots for employers.

From the military? Highlight your discipline, ability to follow standard operating procedures, and experience protecting sensitive information.

From IT? Show off your work with firewalls, account permissions, or endpoint security.

From law enforcement or investigations? Emphasize your evidence handling, chain of custody, and incident investigation skills.

From healthcare? Talk about protecting patient privacy, following HIPAA rules, and working in high-stress, high-stakes environments.

From compliance or auditing? Showcase your understanding of regulations, risk assessments, and reporting.

From academia or other fields? Include research, data analysis, teaching, training, or project management experience.

Step Five – Build Your Personal Roadmap

Your roadmap should answer three simple questions:

Where am I now? Your current skillset and background.

Where do I want to go? Your target role or at least the area of cybersecurity that excites you.

How will I get there? Your plan to close gaps, gain experience, and market yourself for the role. This could include certifications, hands-on labs, volunteering, mentorship, or joining programs like The Lab for real-world practice.

Skipping this step is like wandering into the cybersecurity job market blindfolded. You might stumble into something decent, but more likely you will waste time, energy, and money. Do it right, and you will know exactly which roles to target, which skills to build, and how to position yourself to get hired.

CHAPTER 5:

TRAINING THAT WORKS (WITHOUT WASTING TIME AND MONEY)

If you have been searching for cybersecurity training, you have probably noticed two things.

One, there are more courses, bootcamps, and certifications than there are episodes of *Law & Order*.

Two, everyone claims their program is "all you need" to land a high-paying job in three months or less.

Spoiler alert. It is not.

The right training can be a game-changer. The wrong training can drain your wallet and leave you with a pretty certificate that impresses absolutely no one. Let's talk about how to choose the kind that gets you hired.

Step One – Match Training to Your Goals

If you do not know where you are headed, you will waste time on training that has nothing to do with the role you want. This is why you did the self-assessment in Chapter 4. Now you know your starting point, your gaps, and your target role. That means you can pick training that fills in the missing pieces instead of randomly collecting courses like Pokémon cards.

If you are aiming for SOC or analyst roles, look for hands-on training with SIEM tools like Microsoft Sentinel or Splunk. If you are going toward GRC, focus on risk management frameworks like NIST, ISO 27001, or PCI-DSS. If you want to get into cloud security, invest in AWS, Azure, or Google Cloud certifications.

Step Two – Understand the Certification Game

Certifications can help, but they are not magic keys to the kingdom. Here is the truth about some popular ones:

- CompTIA Security+ – A great starter cert that shows you understand core security concepts.

- CompTIA Network+ – Good if your networking knowledge is weak.

- Certified Ethical Hacker (CEH) – Looks nice on a resume, but employers care more about proven pen testing skills.

- Certified Information Systems Security Professional (CISSP) – More for experienced professionals, not beginners.

- Cloud Certifications (AWS, Azure, GCP) – Must-haves if you are aiming for cloud roles.

Do not collect certs just to "look qualified." Collect them to fill skill gaps that align with the roles you are targeting.

Step Three – Get Real-World Experience Before You Are Hired

You know what impresses employers more than a certification? Proof you have already done the work. That is where hands-on training and labs come in.

You can:

- Build a home lab using free or low-cost tools

- Participate in Capture the Flag (CTF) competitions

- Volunteer with nonprofits that need security help

- Contribute to open-source security projects

And of course, there is **The Lab @ Cyber Boss Consulting** — where you work with real-world tools like Microsoft Sentinel, Defender, and CrowdStrike while being guided by instructors from top companies. By the time you are done, you can talk about actual configurations, investigations, and incident response scenarios you have handled. That is resume gold.

Step Four – Use AI to Make Your Training Smarter

Remember in Chapter 4 when we used AI to figure out where you are? You can also use it to design a training plan.

Prompt example:

> "Act as a cybersecurity career coach. Based on the skills I currently have (list them) and the role I am targeting (name it), create a step-by-step training plan with specific courses, labs, and certifications I should complete in the next six months. Focus on cost-effective options and hands-on learning."

You can run this prompt in ChatGPT or another AI tool to get a tailored plan instead of piecing one together from random YouTube videos and Reddit advice.

Step Five – Avoid Training Traps

Watch out for:

- Overpriced bootcamps that charge $15,000 for content you could find in cheaper programs.

- Cert dumps that teach you to memorize answers instead of understanding the material.

- Lifetime access promises that sound great until you realize you will never go back and watch that 80-hour course again.

The right training is not about the fanciest course or the most letters after your name. It is about building the skills that get you into the field, then growing from there.

Training should be a bridge, not a detour. Get the right skills, get real experience, and then move on to the good stuff, like getting paid to use them.

CHAPTER 6

BUILDING REAL EXPERIENCE BEFORE YOU'RE HIRED

Here is the part nobody tells you when they are selling you a cybersecurity course. Employers want experience. The catch is that you need a job to get experience, but you need experience to get the job. It feels like a bad joke, but there is a way around it. You just have to create your own experience before you are officially hired.

This is where a lot of beginners get stuck. They think if they do not have "Cybersecurity Analyst" in their job history, they have nothing to show. Wrong. You just have to get creative and intentional about where your experience comes from and how you present it.

Step One – Build a Home Lab

A home lab is like your personal cybersecurity playground. You set up systems, break them, secure them, and repeat until you are confident you can do it in a real job.

Your lab can be as simple or complex as you want. You can:

- Install virtual machines on your computer and simulate networks

- Use free tools like Security Onion or Kali Linux for practice

- Run Microsoft Sentinel or Splunk trials to learn SIEM skills

- Practice setting up firewalls, creating user accounts, and applying security patches

Every configuration you do in your lab can be documented as "hands-on project experience" on your resume or LinkedIn. Yes, it counts. If you can talk about it in an interview, it is real experience.

Step Two – Join Competitions and Challenges

Capture the Flag (CTF) competitions, hackathons, and online challenges are among the fastest ways to build technical skills and credibility. You solve security puzzles, analyze logs, crack passwords, and simulate real-world incident response scenarios.

There are platforms like TryHackMe, Hack The Box, and PicoCTF where you can start at the beginner level and work your way up. These challenges do not just teach you; they also give you a public track record you can share with employers.

Step Three – Volunteer or Freelance

Nonprofits, schools, and small businesses often need cybersecurity help but cannot afford full-time staff. Offering your skills in exchange for experience is a win-win. You can help them set up basic protections, perform risk assessments, or train staff on security best practices.

Even small projects like securing a local charity's email system or creating a password policy for a small business give you real stories to share in interviews.

Step Four – Contribute to Open-Source Projects

Open-source security tools and projects are always looking for help, and not just from programmers. You can write documentation, help test new features, or suggest improvements. This shows initiative, teamwork, and technical ability in a collaborative environment.

Step Five – Use The Lab @ Cyber Boss Consulting

Let's be honest. Sometimes self-teaching feels like throwing spaghetti at the wall and hoping something sticks. That is where structured, real-world programs like The Lab come in.

In The Lab, you are not just watching videos. You are:

- Configuring Microsoft Sentinel, Defender, and CrowdStrike

- Analyzing alerts and responding to simulated incidents

- Learning from instructors who do this work every day at companies like Deloitte, Intel, and CGI

- Walking away with documented projects you can list on your resume under "Professional Experience"

That last point is huge. When an employer asks, "Have you ever configured a SIEM?" you can say "Yes" and mean it.

Step Six – Document Everything

This might be the most important part. Document every project, every lab, every competition, and every volunteer gig. Write down what you did, what tools you used, and what results you achieved. This becomes the content for your resume, your LinkedIn profile, and your interview answers.

You do not have to wait for a job offer to start gaining experience. In fact, the more you do before you are hired, the more likely you are to land that first role. Employers are not just looking for people who know the theory. They want people who can get the job done. If you can prove that before day one, you are already ahead of the pack.

PART 3

BRANDING YOURSELF FOR THE INDUSTRY

CHAPTER 7

CRAFTING A CYBERSECURITY RESUME THAT GETS NOTICED

Your resume is your first impression. It is also the thing that decides whether you even get a chance to make a second impression. If it is boring, too long, too vague, or full of fluff, it will get about six seconds of attention before it ends up in the digital trash bin.

The good news? You do not have to be a professional writer to create a resume that makes hiring managers stop scrolling. You have to speak their language, show proof you can do the work, and avoid the rookie mistakes that get 80 percent of resumes ignored.

Step One – Stop Telling, Start Showing

Hiring managers do not care about fancy job titles or long lists of duties. They care about results. Instead of saying "configured security tools," say "configured Microsoft Sentinel to monitor network traffic, reducing false positives by 25 percent."

Numbers and outcomes beat vague buzzwords every time.

Step Two – Put the Good Stuff Up Front

The top third of your resume is prime real estate. This is where you hook them with:

- A strong professional summary that says who you are, what you do, and why they should care.

- A core skills section that lists the technical and soft skills most relevant to the job.

- Key certifications or credentials, if you have them.

Example:

> Professional Summary: Security-minded IT professional transitioning into cybersecurity with hands-on experience in Microsoft Sentinel, CrowdStrike, and network defense. Proven ability to investigate alerts, manage incidents, and communicate findings to technical and non-technical teams.

Step Three – Highlight Hands-On Experience

Remember all the work you did in Chapter 6? This is where you put it to work.

If you built a home lab, list it under Projects or Hands-On Experience:

- Configured a simulated enterprise network with multiple endpoints using Microsoft Sentinel to monitor and respond to alerts.

- Performed penetration testing in a lab environment to identify and patch vulnerabilities using Kali Linux and OWASP ZAP.

If you volunteer, list it under Professional Experience:

- Implemented basic security controls for a nonprofit's email system, reducing phishing incidents by 40 percent.

If you complete **The Lab @ Cyber Boss Consulting**, showcase it like any other job:

- Completed a 12-week real-world cybersecurity apprenticeship training program configuring Microsoft Sentinel, Defender, and CrowdStrike in simulated enterprise environments.

Step Four – Translate Your Past Roles Into Cybersecurity Language

If your past jobs were not in cybersecurity, reframe them so they show transferable skills.

Military? Highlight SOPs, classified information handling, and secure communication protocols.

IT? Emphasize security-related tasks like patch management, account permissions, and firewall configuration.

Healthcare? Focus on protecting sensitive patient data and compliance with HIPAA.

Compliance? Mention audits, risk assessments, and regulatory enforcement.

Law enforcement or investigations? Showcase evidence handling, investigative techniques, and incident reporting.

Step Five – Keep It Clean and Easy to Read

One to two pages max. No complicated layouts, no headshots, and no "creative" fonts that make your resume look like a wedding invitation. Use bullet points, bold key terms, and make sure it is reader friendly.

Step Six – Tailor It for Every Job

Yes, it is extra work. Yes, it is worth it. Read the job posting carefully and make sure your resume reflects the specific tools, skills, and experience they are looking for. If they want Splunk experience and you have it, make sure it is in your summary, skills list, and job descriptions.

Step Seven – Use AI to Make It Stronger

Just like in Chapter 4 and 5, AI can give your resume an instant boost.

Prompt example:

> "Act as a cybersecurity hiring manager. Review my resume and rewrite it so it highlights my relevant skills and experience for a Security Analyst role. Make it results-focused, quantify my achievements where possible, and ensure it matches common industry keywords to pass Applicant Tracking Systems."

You can even paste in a specific job description and ask AI to tailor your resume for that exact role.

A great resume does not just tell someone you want a cybersecurity job. It convinces them you can do the work, and it makes them excited to meet you. Done right, it becomes your ticket from "applicant" to "interviewee," and that is where the real game begins.

CHAPTER 8:

LINKEDIN AND PERSONAL BRANDING

If your resume is your first impression, your LinkedIn profile is the background check before the first date. Recruiters, hiring managers, and even random strangers will look you up before deciding whether you're worth their time. If they find an empty profile that looks like you've been in witness protection, they will move on.

LinkedIn is not just an online resume. Done right, it's your digital storefront, networking hub, and credibility builder all in one. And the best part? You can set it up so it works for you 24/7 without you constantly chasing people.

Building a Profile That Attracts Recruiters

Think of your LinkedIn profile like a billboard. It should answer three questions right away:

1. Who are you?

2. What do you do?

3. Why should anyone care?

Your Headline: This is the first thing recruiters see. Skip "Seeking Opportunities" and write something that sells you:

- *Cybersecurity Apprentice | SOC Analyst in Training | Hands-On Experience with Microsoft Sentinel, Defender, and CrowdStrike*

- *Transitioning from IT to Cybersecurity | GRC Enthusiast | Apprentice in The Lab @ Cyber Boss Consulting*

Your About Section: This is where you tell your story. Keep it short, confident, and focused on what you bring to the table. Mention your transferable skills, your hands-on work, and your career goals.

Your Experience: Do not just list job titles. Use bullet points that describe what you did — especially your Lab apprenticeship. Example:

- Completed a 12-week real-world cybersecurity apprenticeship training program configuring Microsoft Sentinel, Defender, and CrowdStrike in simulated enterprise environments.

Your Skills: Add both technical skills (SIEM, Cloud Security, Incident Response) and soft skills (Problem Solving, Communication, Teamwork). Recruiters use keyword searches, so make sure your skills section is fully stocked.

Content Strategies to Show You're Engaged in the Field

You do not need to post every day, but you should show some signs of life. A "dead" profile looks like you are not serious about the industry.

Easy ways to post:

- Share an article about cybersecurity trends and add your opinion.

- Post about a lab project you completed (screenshots optional).

- Comment thoughtfully on posts from industry leaders.

- Share your wins — new certifications, completed training, competition participation.

🔥 Pro Tip: People engage more with personal stories than with links. Instead of just posting, "I earned my Security+ certification," say, "After months of late-night studying and more practice tests than I can count, I passed my Security+. Here's what I learned along the way…"

Networking Without Feeling Fake

Networking does not mean messaging strangers and asking for a job. It means building relationships so that when opportunities come up, people think of you.

Ways to connect without feeling like a sleazy salesperson:

- Send a short, friendly note with connection requests: "Hi, I'm transitioning into cybersecurity and enjoyed your post on incident response. Would love to connect."

- Join cybersecurity groups and participate in discussions.

- Congratulate people on promotions or career moves.

- Ask genuine questions: "What was your biggest challenge when you started in cybersecurity?" works better than "Can you get me a job?"

Positioning Yourself as a Lab Apprentice to Boost Credibility

Being able to say you are part of The Lab @ Cyber Boss Consulting is a credibility booster.

It shows you are not just studying, you are applying skills in a structured, real-world environment.

Ways to highlight this on LinkedIn:

- Put "Cybersecurity Apprentice" under your Experience section with a description of what you have worked on.

- Add Lab projects under "Projects" with details about the tools and scenarios you worked through.

- Mention your apprenticeship in your About section so it is one of the first things people read.

Example:

> "Currently completing a 12-week cybersecurity apprenticeship in The Lab at Cyber Boss Consulting, gaining hands-on experience in Microsoft Sentinel, Defender, and CrowdStrike, incident response, and security monitoring in simulated enterprise environments."

When you use LinkedIn strategically, you are not chasing opportunities, they start finding you. Recruiters search for keywords, hiring managers check for signs of initiative, and your posts keep you top of mind without feeling pushy. It is networking without the awkward small talk and with the bonus of building your personal brand at the same time.

CHAPTER 9:

BUILDING YOUR PROFESSIONAL NETWORK

Here's the deal. You can have the best resume, the sharpest LinkedIn profile, and every certification under the sun, but if no one in the industry knows you exist, you're playing the job search game on hard mode.

Cybersecurity is a people business as much as it is a tech business. That doesn't mean you have to become a shameless self-promoter or start working the room like a pushy car salesman. It means you need to make genuine connections with people who can open doors, give advice, and help you grow.

Step One – Think Quality Over Quantity

You do not need 5,000 random LinkedIn connections. You need the right people in your circle, those who are active in the field, have credibility, and can offer perspective. This includes:

- Cybersecurity professionals in the roles you want someday

- Recruiters who specialize in security hiring

- Leaders of local or online security groups

- Former classmates, co-workers, or instructors who are already in the industry

If you're in The Lab, your instructor roster alone is a goldmine, these are people from companies like Deloitte, Intel, and CGI who are already in the rooms you want to be in.

Step Two – Join the Right Communities

You don't have to lurk alone in the corner of LinkedIn. There are dozens of places where cybersecurity pros hang out, and many are beginner friendly.

- Local security meetups (check Meetup.com)

- Professional associations like ISACA, ISC2, and ISSA

- Online forums and Slack groups such as Reddit's r/cybersecurity, Blue Team Village, or Threat Hunting Slack

- Conferences like BSides, DEF CON, or regional cyber summits

If the idea of walking into a room full of strangers makes you want to crawl back under the covers, start online. Comment in discussions, share your thoughts, and slowly become a familiar name.

Step Three – Build Relationships, Not Transactions

Networking is not "Hi, I just met you, can you get me a job?" It's about building trust and showing up as a real human being, not a walking request.

Instead of asking for something right away:

- Ask how they got started in the field

- Comment on something they've posted that resonated with you

- Share resources that might help them

- Offer to help with projects, even if it's something small

People remember the ones who bring value before they ask for it.

Step Four – Leverage Your Lab Credibility

When you tell people you're in **The Lab @ Cyber Boss Consulting**, you're telling them you're not just learning theory, you're doing the work. That stands out in a world full of "aspiring cybersecurity analysts" who've never touched a SIEM.

Ways to work this into conversations naturally:

- "I'm currently in a cybersecurity apprenticeship where I configure Sentinel and CrowdStrike in simulated enterprise environments..."

- "In The Lab, I've been working through real-world incident response scenarios..."

This shows you're actively building skills, not just talking about it.

Step Five – Stay in Touch Without Being Annoying

Networking is like gardening. You can't just plant seeds and disappear. Every so often, check in:

- Congratulate them on promotions or job changes

- Share an article you think they'll find interesting

- Update them on your progress and wins

It keeps you on their radar without turning into a spam bot.

The more people who know who you are, what you do, and the value you bring, the more likely opportunities will start finding you instead of you always chasing them. And when your name comes up in the right conversation, you want the person hearing it to say, "Oh yeah, I know them, they'd be a great fit."

PART 4:

LANDING THE JOB

CHAPTER 10:

MASTERING THE CYBERSECURITY JOB HUNT

You have your skills. You have your resume. You have your LinkedIn profile looking sharp.

Now comes the part that makes most people want to pull their hair out: actually, finding and applying for jobs.

The problem is not that there are no jobs. The problem is that there are too many, and half of them are either fake, outdated, or written in a way that makes it look like you need to be a 23-year-old with 15 years of cybersecurity experience.

The good news is that if you know where to look, how to read between the lines, and how to be strategic, you can save yourself a lot of wasted time and get your applications in front of the right people.

The Remote Work Myth

Let's talk about one of the biggest misconceptions out there: the idea that you can land your very first cybersecurity job working from home in your pajamas. Is it possible? Sure. But the truth is, the chances are lower if you have no professional cybersecurity experience. Employers tend to be cautious about giving remote roles to beginners because it takes a certain level of independence, time management, and familiarity with enterprise processes that usually come from working in the field first.

Why? Because remote work in this field requires a level of independence, time management, and familiarity with enterprise processes that most people only learn after being on the job for a while. Companies need to know you can work with a security team, follow incident response procedures, and navigate internal tools, all without someone sitting next to you showing you the ropes.

If you have never worked on a professional cybersecurity team before, they are less likely to take the risk of onboarding you remotely. That is why so many entry-level job seekers get frustrated applying for remote roles and hearing nothing back.

Here's a better strategy: look for local on-site opportunities. In many cases, seasoned professionals avoid on-site jobs because they prefer remote or hybrid setups. This means there is less competition for those roles, giving you a higher chance of getting hired. Once you have some experience under your belt, you will be in a much stronger position to compete for those remote positions.

Where to Find Legitimate Job Postings

If you are still going to Indeed, hitting search, and applying to every job with the word "cybersecurity" in the title, you are doing it wrong. The best jobs are often found in places where there is less competition, and the postings are fresh.

Start with:

- LinkedIn Jobs – Use the filter "posted in last 24 hours" so you are not wasting time on listings that have been sitting there for weeks.

- Company Career Pages – Go directly to the websites of companies you admire and look for openings there.

- Industry-specific job boards – Sites like ClearedJobs.net for security clearance roles, CyberSecJobs.com, InfoSec Jobs, and Dice.

- Professional associations – ISACA, ISC2, and ISSA all have job boards for members.

- Networking leads – Many jobs are never posted publicly. This is where the relationships you built in Chapters 8 and 9 pay off.

🔥 Pro Tip: Always check who posted the job. If it was posted by a recruiter or hiring manager on LinkedIn, connect with them and send a short, professional note. That puts you ahead of the faceless pile of resumes.

How to Read Between the Lines in Job Descriptions

A lot of people see a job posting, notice they do not have 100 percent of the listed requirements, and immediately give up. Here is the secret: job descriptions are often wish lists, not strict checklists.

If you meet about 70 percent of the requirements, apply. Companies will often train the right person if they see potential.

Things to look for:

- Certifications – If they list five, they usually only care about one or two.

- Years of experience – "Three plus years" does not always mean they will reject someone with one year of solid, relevant work.

- Technology lists – You do not need to know every single tool. Show that you have used similar tools and can learn quickly.

- Red flags – Vague descriptions, no salary range, or a job that keeps getting reposted-can be warning signs of high turnover or unclear expectations.

When in doubt, apply and let them decide. Just make sure it is a role you would want.

Applying Strategically Instead of the Spray and Pray Approach

The spray and pray method is when you apply to 50 jobs a day using the same generic resume and cover letter. It feels productive, but it rarely works. Recruiters can tell when they are looking at a mass application.

Instead, focus on quality over quantity:

1. Choose 5 to 10 roles a week that you want.

2. Tailor your resume and cover letter to each role using the keywords and skills from the job description.

3. Look for mutual connections at the company and ask for a referral.

4. Follow the company on LinkedIn and engage with their posts so your name is familiar before they even see your application.

5. Keep a simple spreadsheet to track your applications and follow-ups.

This approach takes more time per application, but your chances of getting interviews will be much higher.

The job hunt is not about applying to the most jobs. It is about applying to the right jobs in the right way, so you are not just another name in a stack of hundreds. Once you focus your efforts, you will spend less time applying and more time talking to people who can hire you.

CHAPTER 11

ACING THE INTERVIEW

The interview is where all the work you have done, building skills, networking, polishing your resume, and fine-tuning your LinkedIn either pays off or falls flat.

For most people, interviews are stressful because they treat them like interrogations.

Interviews are sales conversations, and you are both the salesperson and the product. Your job is to convince them that hiring you will solve their problems and make their lives easier.

Common Cybersecurity Interview Questions (And How to Answer Them)

1. Tell me about yourself. How to answer: Keep it short and focused on your professional background, transferable skills, and why you are in cybersecurity.

    Example:

    > "I started my career in IT where I gained experience managing networks, permissions, and endpoint security. I recently completed a 12-week cybersecurity apprenticeship at The Lab, where I configured Microsoft Sentinel, Defender, and CrowdStrike in a simulated enterprise environment. I also worked on compliance projects using NIST 800-53 and SOC 2 frameworks. I am now looking for a role where I can apply my hands-on skills to help protect critical systems and data."

2. Why do you want to work in cybersecurity? How to answer: Show motivation that goes beyond the paycheck.

   Example:

   > "I enjoy solving complex problems and protecting valuable information. Cybersecurity allows me to combine my technical skills with my interest in risk management and compliance. It is one of the few careers where the work you do can have an immediate and meaningful impact on both an organization and the people it serves."

3. What tools and technologies have you worked with? How to answer: Be specific and include context for when you used each tool.

   Example:

   > "In The Lab, I used Microsoft Sentinel to configure data connectors, create detection rules, and investigate incidents. I worked with Microsoft Defender for endpoint protection and CrowdStrike for advanced threat detection. On the compliance side, I mapped NIST 800-53 controls to SOC 2 requirements using compliance tracking tools. I also implemented role-based access controls in Azure AD and configured network security groups for Azure cloud security."

4. Describe a time you identified and resolved a security issue. How to answer: Use the STAR method — Situation, Task, Action, Result.

   Example:

   > "During my apprenticeship, I was assigned to monitor alerts in Microsoft Sentinel. I identified a series of failed login attempts from an unusual IP range. I investigated the logs, confirmed it was a brute-force attempt,

and isolated the account in question. I implemented conditional access rules in Azure AD to block the IP range and documented the incident for the compliance team. As a result, the simulated enterprise avoided a potential breach."

5. How do you stay up to date with security trends and threats? How to answer: Name credible sources and ongoing practices.

Example:

"I regularly follow threat intelligence blogs like Krebs on Security and Threatpost. I participate in cybersecurity groups on LinkedIn and attend local ISACA and ISSA chapter events. I also work on challenges in Hack The Box and TryHackMe to stay sharp with emerging techniques. In The Lab, we had weekly debriefs on current threats, which helped me connect industry news with real-world defensive strategies."

How to Tell Your Story in a Way That Fits the Role

The best interviews are storytelling sessions with structure. The STAR method (Situation, Task, Action, Result) keeps your answers clear and focused. Employers remember stories better than lists of skills, so give them examples that make them visualize you in the role.

Practical Scenarios and Technical Assessments

Some interviews will include tests like:

- Reviewing a network diagram for vulnerabilities

- Analyzing sample logs to spot suspicious activity

- Walking through a mock incident response

- Writing a short security policy or checklist

These are less about perfection and more about how you think. Talk through your reasoning as you go, it shows confidence and collaboration.

Using The Lab Projects as Proof of Hands-On Ability

When you are new, the hardest thing to prove is that you can do the work. This is where your lab experience becomes your secret weapon.

Here's how you could present it depending on the focus of the role:

Compliance & ISSO Work

> "In my apprenticeship at The Lab, I acted in the role of an Information System Security Officer. I performed a NIST 800-53 moderate baseline review, mapped controls to SOC 2 trust service criteria, and developed remediation plans for access control, incident response, and encryption gaps. I also updated system security plans and created compliance dashboards to track control implementation."

SOC Operations

> "I configured Microsoft Sentinel to collect and correlate logs from multiple endpoints, built custom alert rules, and investigated simulated threats. In one case, I tracked a brute-force login attempt, isolated the affected system, and documented the response in the incident management process."

Identity and Access Management

> "I implemented role-based access control in Azure AD, managed MFA enforcement, and created conditional access rules to align with SOC 2 requirements. I conducted privilege reviews to ensure least-privilege principles were followed."

Azure Cloud Security

"I secured Azure resources by configuring network security groups, enabling Security Center policies, and applying encryption-at-rest for sensitive data. I ran compliance scans to ensure alignment with NIST 800-53 system and communications protection controls."

Program Development

"I designed a security awareness training program that included phishing simulations, monthly training modules, and metrics reporting. This program was aligned with NIST awareness and training controls and SOC 2 security awareness requirements."

The interview is not about proving you know everything, it is about proving you can learn quickly, work with a team, and apply your skills in real situations. When you walk in with specific examples, especially ones grounded in hands-on lab work, you turn "I studied this" into "I have already done this." That is what gets you an offer.

CHAPTER 12:

NEGOTIATING YOUR FIRST OFFER

Congratulations. You made it. You have gone from learning the ropes to getting an offer on the table. Now comes the part that makes a lot of people nervous: talking about money.

The problem is most beginners either accept the first number they hear or get so caught up in trying to negotiate like a pro that they overplay their hand and lose the opportunity. The goal here is balance. You want to make sure you are paid fairly, but you also want to think about the bigger picture and where this role will take you.

Understanding Market Rates

Before you start throwing out numbers, you need to know what the market is paying for your role in your area. Salaries for cybersecurity positions can vary wildly depending on location, industry, and company size.

To figure out what is realistic:

- Check sites like Glassdoor, Payscale, and Salary.com for your job title and location.

- Look at LinkedIn job postings that list salary ranges.

- Ask trusted contacts in your network what is typical for entry-level roles in your area.

If you have additional skills or certifications (and especially hands-on lab experience), you can push toward the higher end of the range. But if you are truly at the beginning of your cybersecurity career, do not expect to get top dollar just yet.

Negotiating Salary, Benefits, and Growth Opportunities

When the offer comes in, thank them and ask for time to review. This gives you a chance to assess the full package.

Salary matters, but so do the extras:

- Training and certification budgets: Can you get Security+, CISSP, or cloud certs paid for?

- Professional development: Will they send you to conferences or workshops?

- Work schedule: Is there flexibility for hybrid work later?

- Growth path: Is there a clear way to move into more advanced roles?

You can negotiate more than just the paycheck. If they are firm on salary, ask for additional benefits like paid training, a signing bonus, or an earlier performance review to revisit pay.

When you make your counteroffer, be respectful and back it up with reasons.

For example:

> "Based on my research of similar roles in this area and the hands-on experience I gained in my apprenticeship with The Lab, I believe a salary of $XX, XXX would be a fair reflection of the value I can bring."

When to Take a Lower Offer for Strategic Career Growth

Sometimes the smartest career move is to take an offer that is not the highest paying. This is especially true if:

- The role gives you significant hands-on experience with tools and responsibilities you can leverage later.

- You will be working with strong mentors who can accelerate your learning.

- The company has a track record of promoting from within.

- The position fills a gap in your experience that is blocking you from your next career step.

Think of your first cybersecurity job as a launchpad. If it sets you up for a higher-paying and more specialized role in 12 to 18 months, it is worth considering even if the paycheck is smaller right now.

The key to negotiating your first offer is to think strategically. You are not just negotiating for today; you are setting the tone for your career trajectory. Be informed, be confident, and be willing to take the long view if it gets you where you really want to go.

PART 5:

THRIVING AFTER YOU'RE IN

CHAPTER 13

THE FIRST 90 DAYS

You got the offer; you signed the paperwork, and now it is game time. The first three months in your new cybersecurity role are critical. This is when you set the tone for your reputation, your relationships, and your long-term growth at the company.

A lot of people walk in thinking, "I just need to keep my head down and not mess up." But the truth is, the first 90 days are your chance to prove that the company made the right choice in hiring you.

How to Make a Strong Impression Quickly

You do not have to know everything on day one. What you do have to show is that you are curious, dependable, and coachable.

- Show up prepared: Review any onboarding materials ahead of time and make sure your accounts and access are set up as soon as possible.

- Ask smart questions: Not "What does this button do?" but "Can you walk me through how our incident escalation process works?"

- Take notes: You will not remember everything you are told. Write it down. This shows you are serious about learning.

- Be proactive: Volunteer for tasks you feel comfortable tackling, even if they are small. Small wins early on build trust.

Your goal is not to impress them with how much you know, but to show that you are reliable, engaged, and willing to learn fast.

Building Relationships with Your Team

Cybersecurity is a team sport. You will be working with SOC analysts, engineers, compliance officers, IT staff, and sometimes even legal and HR.

- Introduce yourself: A short "Hi, I'm new here" goes a long way.

- Find your go-to people: There will be teammates who are especially helpful and patient. Connect with them early.

- Be visible: If you are hybrid or on-site, do not hide behind your desk. Join team meetings, participate in discussions, and show up for group activities.

- Show appreciation: Thank people when they help you. It builds goodwill fast.

Balancing Learning and Delivering Results

In your first 90 days, you are both a student and a contributor. That means finding the balance between absorbing information and doing the work.

- Set learning goals: Maybe it is getting fully comfortable with your SIEM tool by week six or completing compliance training in the first month.

- Deliver on commitments: If you say you will get something done, get it done. Nothing builds trust faster.

- Ask for feedback early: Do not wait for your 90-day review to find out if you are on track.

Remember, your goal is not perfection. It is progress. You are building a foundation for long-term success.

Continuing Access to The Lab Instructor for Ongoing Support

While your Lab apprenticeship officially ends once you complete the program, you do have the option of keeping a direct line to your instructor for ongoing support. For $99 a month, you can maintain access to your Lab instructor to ask questions, get clarity on concepts, or troubleshoot configuration issues you might run into in your new role.

This is not full access to the Lab environment, but it is the next best thing, having an experienced industry professional in your corner.

- Configuration help: If you are setting up Microsoft Sentinel rules, Azure AD policies, or IAM roles at work and run into trouble, you can get guidance before making costly mistakes.

- Quick answers: Instead of spending hours digging through forums, you can get reliable, real-world advice tailored to your situation.

- Confidence boost: Knowing you have an expert to turn to helps you take on new responsibilities without second-guessing yourself.

This kind of ongoing mentorship can be the difference between slowly figuring things out on your own and accelerating your growth in the field.

The first 90 days are not about proving you are perfect. They are about proving you are worth investing in. Show you can learn fast, work well with others, and deliver results, and you will set yourself up for long-term success in the company and in your career.

CHAPTER 14

LEVELING UP

You have survived your first 90 days, settled into your role, and proven you can do the work. Now what?

This is where a lot of people make the mistake of getting comfortable. They show up, do their job, and wait for someone to notice and hand them a promotion. That is not how it works. Promotions, specialty roles, and high-impact opportunities usually go to the people who make themselves impossible to ignore, the ones who consistently bring value, learn new skills, and step up before being asked.

How to Position Yourself for Promotion or Specialization

If you want to move up, you must start acting like the person who already belongs in that next role.

- Ask for more responsibility: Volunteer for projects slightly outside your current role. This shows initiative and gives you a track record you can point to when asking for a promotion.

- Solve problems others avoid: If something is broken and everyone is ignoring it, be the one to fix it or at least propose a solution.

- Document your wins: Keep a running list of projects you completed, incidents you resolved, compliance audits you helped pass, or efficiencies you created. When promotion time comes, you will have proof.

- Align with company goals: If leadership is focused on cloud migration, security automation, or compliance certification, position yourself as someone who can contribute directly to those priorities.

Continual Learning Strategies

Cybersecurity changes faster than most industries. What you learned a year ago may already be outdated. If you stop learning, you stop growing.

- Certifications with purpose: Do not collect certs just to have them. Choose ones that align with the role you want next, like CISSP for leadership, CCSP for cloud security, or CISM for management.

- Hands-on practice: Spin up your own lab at home or use platforms like TryHackMe and Hack The Box. The more you practice, the more confident you become.

- Follow industry news: Subscribe to security blogs, join online forums, and attend webinars so you are aware of new threats, regulations, and tools.

- Mentorship: Find someone in your desired specialty or leadership track who can guide you. Even one conversation a month can accelerate your growth.

Moving into Leadership or Niche Roles

Once you have a few years of solid experience, you will face a choice: move into leadership or become a specialist. Both paths have their rewards.

Leadership Path – You move into roles like Team Lead, Security Manager, or CISO. Your focus shifts from hands-on technical work to strategy, budgeting, risk management, and leading teams. This path often comes with higher pay but also more responsibility and less time "in the weeds" technically.

Specialist Path – You deepen your expertise in a specific area, like penetration testing, cloud security, identity and access management, digital forensics, or compliance (NIST, SOC 2, PCI-DSS). Specialists are in high demand because they can solve problems most people cannot.

🔥 Pro Tip: Even if you choose the specialist path, develop basic leadership skills. The ability to manage projects, communicate clearly, and mentor others will set you apart from other technical experts.

Starting Your Own Cybersecurity Firm

If you have developed expertise, built a network, and identified a gap in the market, starting your own cybersecurity business might be the ultimate level-up.

- Find your niche: You could focus on compliance consulting, SOC-as-a-Service, penetration testing, or managed security services.

- Leverage your network: Your past colleagues, clients, and mentors can be your first customers or referral sources.

- Know the business side: Technical skills alone are not enough. Learn about contracts, marketing, finance, and client management.

- Start small and scale: Begin with one or two service offerings and grow as you build credibility and revenue.

Acquiring Government Contracts

Government contracts can be lucrative and long-term, but they require preparation and persistence.

- Register as a federal contractor – Use SAM.gov to create your profile.

- Get the right certifications – Depending on your business, you might need to comply with FedRAMP, CMMC, or NIST 800-171.

- Search for opportunities – Federal, state, and local governments post RFPs (Requests for Proposal) on public sites.

- Leverage set-aside programs – If you qualify as a minority-owned, woman-owned, veteran-owned, or small disadvantaged business, there are contract opportunities reserved for you.

- Start with subcontracting – Partner with larger prime contractors to get your foot in the door before bidding directly.

Founding New Technologies

Some of the biggest names in cybersecurity started with an idea that solved a problem no one else had addressed.

- Identify an unmet need – Pay attention to the pain points in your day-to-day work. If you keep saying, "There should be a tool for this," you might be onto something.

- Prototype and test – Build a minimal viable product (MVP) and test it with a small group of trusted peers.

- Seek funding and partnerships – Once you prove the concept works, you can attract investors or strategic partners.

- Protect your intellectual property – Consider patents, trademarks, and copyrights to secure your innovation.

Innovation is a level-up because it positions you not just as a practitioner, but as a creator who is shaping the industry.

Leveling up is not just about getting a better title. It is about intentionally building a career that matches your strengths, interests, and lifestyle goals. That could mean climbing the ladder inside a company, becoming the go-to specialist in your field, building your own business, securing high-value contracts, or creating technology that changes how cybersecurity is done.

If you keep learning, keep delivering value, and keep making yourself visible, the next opportunity will not just find you, you will be ready for it.

CHAPTER 15:

GIVING BACK TO THE COMMUNITY

By this point, you have built a career, sharpened your skills, and positioned yourself for growth. Now it is time to look beyond your own success and think about how you can make an impact on others.

Giving back is not just a nice thing to do. It is one of the smartest ways to build your reputation, expand your network, and stay relevant in an industry that changes faster than almost any other.

Mentorship, Teaching, and Public Speaking

If you have ever had someone open a door for you in your career, you already know the value of mentorship. Now you can be that person for someone else.

- Mentorship – Offer to guide newcomers through their first months in the field. This could be as formal as joining an official mentorship program, or as informal as checking in with someone once a month.

- Teaching – Run workshops, lead training sessions at your company, or volunteer to teach basic security practices at schools or community organizations.

- Public Speaking – Share your expertise at conferences, webinars, or local meetups. You do not need to be a world-famous expert to present. just share your real-world experience and lessons learned.

🔥 Pro Tip: Every time you teach or speak, you are also reinforcing your own knowledge.

Helping Others Transition into Cybersecurity

Remember how it felt starting out, overwhelmed, confused, and wondering if you even belonged here? You can change that for someone else.

Ways to help:

- Share your story – Post on LinkedIn about your career path, the obstacles you faced, and what helped you succeed.

- Review resumes – Offer feedback to job seekers who want to break in.

- Host Q&A sessions – Answer questions from aspiring cybersecurity professionals in online forums or community groups.

- Connect people to resources – Point them toward quality training programs, study groups, or networking opportunities.

When you help others grow, you build a reputation as a trusted and generous professional. People remember that.

Staying Relevant in a Constantly Evolving Field

Cybersecurity never stands still, and giving back keeps you plugged into the latest trends, tools, and threats.

When you mentor, you get fresh perspectives from people just entering the field. When you teach, you must stay current so that your knowledge is valuable. When you speak publicly, you naturally push yourself to be up to date so you can answer questions with confidence.

The more active you are in the community, the more likely you are to hear about new opportunities, learn emerging best practices, and spot industry shifts before they happen.

The Payoff of Giving Back

Giving back is not just about what you do for others, it's about what it does for you. You strengthen your professional brand; you build deeper relationships, and you create a network that will be there when you need it most.

And here is the best part: the same way someone once helped you, you now get to pass that on. In an industry as important as cybersecurity, that is not just a nice gesture, it is part of our responsibility to the next generation of defenders.

EPILOGUE

Your Next Move Starts Now

You have made it to the end of this book, but this is only the beginning. You now have the roadmap in your hands, a clear set of steps, resources, and strategies to move from where you are today to where you want to be in your cybersecurity career.

The truth is, most people will read a book like this, feel inspired, and then go right back to doing nothing. That is not going to be you. You did not spend the time going through these chapters just to stay stuck in the same place.

You Know Enough to Start

You might not know everything yet, but you know enough to take the first step, and that is all you need right now.

- If you are still figuring out your path, go back to your skills inventory and choose a starting point.

- If you already know your direction, begin building your first project, lab, or certification plan today.

- If you are ready for the job hunt, polish your resume and LinkedIn and start applying strategically.

Do Not Wait for Permission

No one is going to tap you on the shoulder and say, "It's time to start your cybersecurity career." You must decide for yourself. The industry is hungry for skilled, driven people. Every day you wait is another day someone else steps into the role that could have been yours.

Keep Learning, Keep Building, Keep Connecting

Your career will be built on three pillars:

1. Skills: Keep leveling them up through labs, certifications, and real-world practice.

2. Experience: Document every project, every incident, and every success.

3. Network: Stay connected to peers, mentors, and industry groups. Opportunities live in relationships.

The Lab Is Still Here for You

If you ever get stuck, need clarity, or run into challenges on the job, remember that you can still have direct access to your Lab instructor for $99 a month. You do not have to navigate this alone; support is there when you need it.

Your Blueprint Is Now a To-Do List

Everything in this book is actionable. The chapters are not just information, they are instructions. Go through them again, one at a time, and turn each piece of advice into a task you can check off.

Final Thought: Cybersecurity is not just a career. It is an opportunity to make an impact, protect what matters, and build a future that is both rewarding and secure. You have the tools, the plan, and the capability. Now it is time to act.

Your next move starts today.

ABOUT THE AUTHOR

Danielle Robinson is the Founder and CEO of **Cyber Boss Consulting**, where she serves as a trusted vCISO and advisor to organizations across healthcare, government, and critical infrastructure. With years of experience helping businesses strengthen their defenses and meet strict compliance standards such as NIST, HIPAA, and PCI-DSS, Danielle brings both technical expertise and a strategic perspective to the ever-evolving world of cybersecurity.

Passionate about creating opportunities for others, she founded **The Lab @ Cyber Boss Consulting**, an apprenticeship-style program that gives students, veterans, and IT professionals the hands-on training they need to break into the field. Danielle's work has empowered countless professionals to launch and grow their cybersecurity careers with confidence.

When she is not advising companies or mentoring the next generation of cybersecurity leaders, Danielle is writing, speaking, and developing resources that make cybersecurity accessible, practical, and actionable for all.

BONUS RESOURCES

CYBERSECURITY CERTIFICATION ROADMAP

Certifications are not magic keys to a high-paying job, but they can open doors, especially when you choose the right ones at the right time. This roadmap is designed to give you a logical progression, so you do not waste time (or money) on certifications that do not match your career stage or goals.

Step 1 – Foundation Level (0 to 1 Year Experience)

If you are brand new to cybersecurity, start with certifications that cover the basics and prove you have a solid understanding of security concepts.

- CompTIA IT Fundamentals (ITF+) – Optional if you have zero tech background and want to learn the basics of hardware, software, and networking.

- CompTIA A+ – Good for those coming from help desk or tech support into security.

- CompTIA Network+ – Provides a strong networking foundation, which is critical for all security roles.

- CompTIA Security+ – Often the first "real" security certification employers look for in entry-level candidates.

Goal: Build core IT and security knowledge so you can transition into entry-level security roles like SOC Analyst Tier 1 or Junior Security Specialist.

Step 2 – Early Career Specialization (1 to 3 Years Experience)

Once you have the basics and some real-world experience, start focusing on certifications that align with your desired career path.

- SOC / Blue Team Path – CompTIA CySA+ (Cybersecurity Analyst), Microsoft Security Operations Analyst (SC-200).

- Penetration Testing / Red Team Path – eJPT (eLearnSecurity Junior Penetration Tester), CompTIA Pentest+, Offensive Security Certified Professional (OSCP).

- Cloud Security Path – Microsoft Certified: Azure Security Engineer Associate, AWS Certified Security Specialty, Google Professional Cloud Security Engineer.

- GRC / Compliance Path – Certified Information Systems Auditor (CISA), Certified in Risk and Information Systems Control (CRISC).

Goal: Strengthen skills in your chosen specialty so you can move into mid-level positions.

Step 3 – Advanced and Leadership Roles (3+ Years Experience)

At this stage, you are moving into senior or leadership positions, and certifications should reflect deep expertise or strategic oversight skills.

- Leadership / Management – Certified Information Systems Security Professional (CISSP), Certified Information Security Manager (CISM).

- Advanced Technical Roles – GIAC Security Expert (GSE), Offensive Security Experienced Penetration Tester (OSEP).

- Specialized Areas – GIAC Certified Incident Handler (GCIH), GIAC Cloud Security Essentials (GCLD), GIAC Security Leadership (GSLC).

Goal: Establish authority in your field and qualify for higher-level roles like Senior Security Engineer, Security Manager, or CISO.

Step 4 – Continuous Learning

Certifications expire or become outdated, so make renewal and ongoing education part of your plan. Also, remember that hands-on experience is just as valuable, if not more valuable, than any piece of paper.

- Stay active in labs, simulations, and competitions.

- Pair each certification with real-world projects so you can speak to your experience in interviews.

- Keep an eye on emerging certifications in cloud, AI security, and compliance frameworks.

🔥 Pro Tip: Do not get caught in "certification collecting." Pick certs that directly advance your career goals, fill a gap in your skills, or make you competitive for a specific role you want. The right cert at the right time is powerful. The wrong cert at the wrong time is just expensive wall art.

FREE LABS & PRACTICE ENVIRONMENTS

Hands-on practice is one of the fastest ways to build real cybersecurity skills and have something tangible to talk about in interviews. The good news is you do not need to spend thousands of dollars on fancy lab environments to start, there are plenty of free resources that can help you gain real-world experience right from your own laptop.

General Cybersecurity Practice

- TryHackMe (Free Tier) – Guided, beginner-friendly security labs covering everything from SOC operations to penetration testing. Paid tiers available for advanced content. https://tryhackme.com

- Hack The Box (Free Tier) – Realistic hacking challenges and vulnerable machines to test your skills. Stronger focus on offensive security but good for general problem-solving. https://www.hackthebox.com

- OverTheWire – Wargame-style challenges that teach Linux basics, scripting, and security concepts through hands-on puzzles. https://overthewire.org

- CyberDefenders – Blue team-focused platform with free threat hunting, incident response, and SOC analyst challenges. https://cyberdefenders.org

Cloud Security Labs

- Microsoft Learn – Free Azure sandbox environments tied to specific training modules. Great for practicing cloud security and identity management. https://learn.microsoft.com/training

- AWS Skill Builder (Free Tier) – Labs and training modules with AWS services, including security configurations and IAM practice. https://aws.amazon.com/training

- Google Cloud Skills Boost (Free Tier) – Cloud security labs and projects using Google Cloud's security tools. https://cloudskillsboost.google

SOC, SIEM, and Blue Team Labs

- Splunk Boss of the SOC (BOTS) – Downloadable datasets and challenges to practice searching logs and investigating incidents. https://www.splunk.com/en_us/blog/security/bots.html

- Security Blue Team Free Labs – Hands-on incident response, network traffic analysis, and SIEM usage. https://securityblue.team

- AlienVault OSSIM – Free open-source SIEM you can install and experiment with in a home lab. https://cybersecurity.att.com/products/ossim

Digital Forensics and Incident Response (DFIR)

- Volatility Memory Forensics Labs – Free datasets and practice cases to analyze using Volatility framework. https://volatilityfoundation.org

- DFIR Training Free Resources – Guides and challenges for disk, memory, and network forensic analysis. https://dfir.training

Vulnerability Scanning and Exploitation

- VulnHub – Downloadable vulnerable machines you can run locally in VirtualBox or VMware for exploitation practice. https://www.vulnhub.com

- Metasploitable 2 – A deliberately vulnerable Linux VM from Rapid7 for Metasploit practice. https://sourceforge.net/projects/metasploitable/

🔥 Pro Tip: Document everything you do in these labs, screenshots, configurations, and write-ups. Those notes become "project experience" you can add to your resume and talk about in interviews.

RESUME & LINKEDIN PROFILE TEMPLATES

When you are starting in cybersecurity, it is not enough to just list your past jobs. You must present your experience, skills, and training in a way that connects directly to what employers are looking for. These templates give you a proven structure that is recruiter-friendly and easy to customize for your own background.

Cybersecurity Resume Template (1–2 Pages)

[Full Name] [City, State] | [Email] | [Phone] | [LinkedIn URL] | [Portfolio or GitHub URL]

Professional Summary Brief 3–4 sentence overview that highlights your background, core skills, and cybersecurity career goal. Focus on what makes you a strong candidate for the role.

Example:

> Cybersecurity professional with hands-on experience in security operations, compliance frameworks, and cloud security through a 12-week apprenticeship at The Lab, Cyber Boss Consulting. Skilled in Microsoft Sentinel, Defender, CrowdStrike, and Azure AD. Adept at incident investigation, access control management, and aligning security controls with NIST 800-53 and SOC 2 requirements.

Core Skills

- Security Information and Event Management (SIEM) – Microsoft Sentinel, Splunk

- Endpoint Protection – Microsoft Defender, CrowdStrike

- Cloud Security – Azure AD, Conditional Access, Network Security Groups

- Compliance – NIST 800-53, SOC 2, Security Awareness Training

- Incident Response – Log Analysis, Threat Hunting, Alert Triage

- Tools – Wireshark, Nessus, PowerShell, Python

Professional Experience Cybersecurity Apprentice – The Lab, Cyber Boss Consulting | Dates

- Completed 12-week real-world cybersecurity apprenticeship training program configuring Microsoft Sentinel, Defender, and CrowdStrike in simulated enterprise environments.

- Conducted compliance assessments using NIST 800-53 moderate baseline and SOC 2 trust service criteria; created remediation plans for identified gaps.

- Investigated simulated incidents, including phishing attempts and brute-force attacks, documenting findings and recommended mitigations.

- Implemented Azure AD role-based access control, MFA enforcement, and conditional access rules to meet compliance requirements.

[Previous Role Title] – [Company Name] | Dates

- Translate your past experience into security-related accomplishments.

- Highlight transferable skills such as system administration, IT support, compliance, or process improvement.

Education & Certifications

- [Degree or Program], [School Name], [Year]

- CompTIA Security+ | Azure Security Engineer Associate | [Other Relevant Certs]

Projects (*Optional*)

- Threat Hunting Simulation: Configured Sentinel queries to identify suspicious login activity.

- Security Awareness Program: Developed and delivered training aligned with NIST requirements.

LinkedIn Profile Template

Profile Photo Use a professional headshot with good lighting and a neutral background.

Headline Combine your role, specialty, and key skills. Example: *Cybersecurity Apprentice | SOC Analyst in Training | Hands-On Microsoft Sentinel, Defender, and CrowdStrike*

About Section A short, engaging summary written in first person. Example:

I help organizations protect their data and systems by combining technical skills with a compliance-focused mindset. During my 12-week apprenticeship at The Lab, Cyber Boss Consulting, I worked on security operations, Azure cloud security, and aligning controls with NIST 800-53 and SOC 2. I am passionate about incident response, identity and access management, and creating security programs that strengthen an organization's defenses.

Experience List your cybersecurity apprenticeship first, then any past roles that connect to security, even indirectly. Use bullet points from your resume but keep them concise.

Skills Section Add relevant technical and soft skills. Aim for 30–50 skills so you show up in recruiter searches.

Featured Section (*Optional*) Link to any public projects, blogs, certifications, or portfolios you have.

🔥 Pro Tip: Once you build these templates out, run them through AI or a trusted mentor for feedback and keyword optimization. Every job posting will have slightly different terms and tools listed, tweak your resume and LinkedIn profile each time so they match the role you are targeting.

INTERVIEW PREPARATION CHECKLIST & USING AI

Walking in an interview unprepared is like walking into a boxing ring without gloves. You are hoping you don't get knocked out. The right preparation can turn interview anxiety into confidence. This checklist covers what to do before, during, and after your interview, plus how to use AI to give you an edge.

Interview Preparation Checklist

1. Research the Company and Role

- Learn about the company's industry, products, and services.

- Read recent news or press releases to understand their priorities and challenges.

- Review the job description and highlight the required skills, tools, and responsibilities.

2. Review Your Resume and Lab Projects

- Be ready to explain every bullet point on your resume.

- Have 3–5 detailed examples from The Lab, your home lab, or past roles that show your skills in action.

- Practice telling stories using the STAR method (Situation, Task, Action, Result).

3. Brush Up on Technical Knowledge

- Review the tools and technologies listed in the job description (SIEM, cloud platforms, IAM, compliance frameworks).

- Be ready to walk through a sample incident response, security control implementation, or cloud configuration.

4. Prepare for Common Cybersecurity Interview Questions

- "Tell me about yourself."

- "Describe a security incident you worked on."

- "How do you stay up to date with threats?"

- "Explain [tool or framework] and how you have used it."

5. Practice Behavioral Questions

- "Tell me about a time you solved a problem under pressure."

- "Describe a time you worked with a difficult team member."

- "Give an example of how you prioritized multiple urgent tasks."

6. Plan Your Questions for Them Good questions make you look engaged and informed. Examples:

- "How does the security team measure success here?"

- "What tools or frameworks will I be working with most often?"

- "What training or growth opportunities are available?"

7. Set Up for Success on Interview Day

- For virtual interviews: Test your camera, microphone, and internet.

- For in-person: Arrive 10–15 minutes early.

- Dress one step more formal than the company's dress code.

- Bring copies of your resume and a notebook.

8. Follow Up After the Interview

- Send a thank-you email within 24 hours.

- Reiterate your interest and highlight one key thing you enjoyed discussing.

Using AI to Prepare Like a Pro

AI tools like ChatGPT can help you prepare faster, anticipate questions, and polish your answers. Here are ways to make it work for you:

1. Create a Customized Question Bank

   Prompt:

   > "Act as a cybersecurity hiring manager for a [SOC Analyst / GRC Specialist / Cloud Security Engineer / ISSO] role. Generate a list of 20 interview questions, 10 technical and 10 behavioral, based on this job description: [paste job description]."

2. Get Feedback on Your Answers

   Prompt:

   > "Here is my answer to the question 'Tell me about yourself.' Please rewrite it to be concise, confident, and aligned with the skills in this job description: [paste answer and job description]."

3. Practice Mock Interviews

   Prompt:

   > "Act as a cybersecurity interviewer for a [specific role]. Ask me one question at a time, wait for my answer, then give me feedback and a sample improved answer."

4. Research the Company Faster

    Prompt:

    > "Summarize the most recent cybersecurity-related news and initiatives for [company name] from the past 12 months."

5. Turn Your Lab Experience into Interview Stories

    Prompt:

    > "I completed the following cybersecurity projects in an apprenticeship at The Lab: [list projects]. Rewrite them into STAR method interview answers that emphasize results and impact."

🔥 Pro Tip: AI should be a tool, not a crutch. Use it to prepare and refine your answers, but practice delivering them naturally, so you do not sound rehearsed or robotic in the interview.

BONUS: NETWORKING & PROFESSIONAL GROUP DIRECTORY

The right network can do more for your career than a dozen cold applications. Professional groups, associations, and meetups are where you build relationships, find mentors, and hear about opportunities before they are posted online.

Below is a directory of some of the best places, online and in person, to start building those connections.

Global & National Cybersecurity Organizations

- (ISC)² – Offers certifications like CISSP and SSCP, plus local chapters for networking and events. https://www.isc2.org

- ISACA – Known for CISM, CRISC, and CISA certifications; active local chapters; and governance and risk focus. https://www.isaca.org

- InfraGard – Partnership between the FBI and the private sector focused on critical infrastructure protection. https://www.infragard.org

- Information Systems Security Association (ISSA) – Professional association with chapters worldwide offering networking, events, and training. https://www.issa.org

- Women in CyberSecurity (WiCyS) – Global community supporting women in cybersecurity through networking, mentorship, and conferences. https://www.wicys.org

Specialized Interest Groups

- Cloud Security Alliance (CSA) – Community and research for cloud security best practices. https://cloudsecurityalliance.org

- Open Web Application Security Project (OWASP) – Focused on application security with open-source projects and local chapters worldwide. https://owasp.org

- SANS CyberTalent Immersion Academies – Training and networking opportunities for those entering the field. https://www.sans.org/cybertalent

- Defcon Groups – Local meetups for hacking and security enthusiasts, affiliated with the DEF CON conference. https://defcongroups.org

Government & Military Affiliated Networks

- Military Cyber Professionals Association (MCPA) – Networking and resources for military-affiliated cybersecurity professionals. https://www.milcyber.org

- National Initiative for Cybersecurity Careers and Studies (NICCS) – US government resource for training, events, and career tools. https://niccs.cisa.gov

Local Meetups & Community Groups

- Meetup.com Cybersecurity Groups – Search for cybersecurity, ethical hacking, or cloud security meetups in your city. https://www.meetup.com

- BSides Conferences – Community-driven security conferences held in cities worldwide, affordable and beginner-friendly. https://www.securitybsides.com

- Toastmasters for Tech Professionals – Not security-specific, but great for developing public speaking and leadership skills that can boost your cyber career. https://www.toastmasters.org

Online-Only Networking & Discussion Forums

- LinkedIn Cybersecurity Groups – Join groups like "Cybersecurity Professionals" and "Information Security Community" to connect with peers and recruiters. https://www.linkedin.com/groups

- Reddit Communities – r/cybersecurity, r/netsec, r/AskNetsec for discussions, advice, and industry news. https://www.reddit.com

- Cybersecurity Discord Servers – Many free servers offer real-time chat, mentoring, and job postings. Search "cybersecurity Discord" for open communities.

🔥 Pro Tip: Do not just join, participate. Comment on discussions, attend events, and follow up with people you meet. Relationships are built through consistent interaction, not just by adding your name to a membership list.

THE LAB'S "GETTING STARTED IN CYBERSECURITY" TOOLKIT

Breaking into cybersecurity can feel overwhelming, so many tools to learn, frameworks to understand, and career paths to choose from. The Lab's "Getting Started in Cybersecurity" Toolkit is designed to cut through the noise and give you a focused, actionable starting point.

This is the same roadmap and set of resources our Lab apprentices use to gain hands-on skills, align with industry standards, and position themselves for in-demand roles.

1. The Cybersecurity Career Quick-Start Guide

- Role Profiles – SOC Analyst, GRC Specialist, Cloud Security Engineer, Identity & Access Management (IAM) Specialist, Penetration Tester.

- Skill Requirements – Core technical, compliance, and soft skills for each role.

- Entry Points – Which roles are beginner-friendly and which require more experience.

- Career Path Planning – How to move from entry-level to mid-level and eventually into leadership or niche specialties.

2. Hands-On Learning Blueprint

- Home Lab Setup Guide – How to set up virtual machines, install free security tools, and simulate a secure enterprise environment on your own computer.

- Free Lab Platforms – TryHackMe, Hack The Box, CyberDefenders, Microsoft Learn sandboxes, and more.

- Step-by-Step Practice Tracks – Beginner (security fundamentals), Intermediate (incident response, SIEM), Advanced (cloud security, compliance program builds).

3. Framework & Compliance Starter Pack

- NIST 800-53 Quick Reference Sheet – Control families explained in plain English.

- SOC 2 Readiness Checklist – Core trust service criteria and common gaps.

- Mapping Exercise – How to link technical tasks (like configuring a SIEM) to compliance requirements (like audit logging and monitoring).

4. The Essential Tools List

Free or affordable tools to start practicing right away:

- SOC Tools – Microsoft Sentinel (trial), Splunk (free), Security Onion.

- Endpoint Protection – Microsoft Defender (enterprise trial), CrowdStrike Falcon (trial).

- Cloud Security – Azure AD, AWS IAM free tier, Google Cloud IAM.

- Vulnerability Scanning – Nessus Essentials, OpenVAS.

- Investigation & Analysis – Wireshark, Volatility, Autopsy.

5. Resume & LinkedIn Jumpstart Kit

- Cybersecurity Resume Template – Optimized for Applicant Tracking Systems (ATS).

- LinkedIn Headline & Summary Examples – Tailored for new cybersecurity professionals.

- Project-to-Resume Translation Guide – How to turn Lab, home lab, or volunteer work into resume bullets that get interviews.

6. Interview Prep Pack

- 20 Common Cybersecurity Interview Questions – With sample answers based on Lab experience.

- STAR Method Worksheet – Fill-in-the-blank prompts to turn your projects into compelling stories.

- AI-Powered Mock Interview Script – Prompts you can use with ChatGPT to simulate interviews for specific roles.

7. The $99/Month Instructor Support Option *(Optional)*

After you finish The Lab, you can choose to keep direct access to your instructor for ongoing Q&A and troubleshooting. Perfect for when you start your first job and need quick, reliable answers to real-world challenges. Inquire today!

How to Use This Toolkit

1. Pick Your Target Role – Don't try to learn everything at once.

2. Follow the Hands-On Learning Blueprint – Build your skills through labs and projects.

3. Map Your Work to Compliance – Learn to connect technical actions to business and audit requirements.

4. Document Everything – Your lab work becomes your "experience" in interviews.

5. Network & Apply – Use the resume, LinkedIn, and networking strategies from earlier chapters.

🔥 Pro Tip: This toolkit works best when you give yourself a timeline. Dedicate 8–12 weeks to going through each section, and by the end, you will have the skills, documentation, and confidence to land your first cybersecurity role.

EXCLUSIVE BONUS FOR READERS

Thank you for purchasing *Cybersecurity Career Blueprint: Fast-Tracking Your Way to Success*. As a reader, you get access to The Lab's "Getting Started in Cybersecurity" Toolkit. The same roadmap and resources our apprentices use to build real skills and break into the field.

To claim your free copy:
📧 Send an email with your proof of purchase to support@ cyberbossconsulting.com.
⏱️ Once verified, your toolkit will be delivered straight to your inbox within 24–48 hours.

This bonus resource is designed to give you a clear, actionable starting point so you can take the strategies from this book and put them into practice right away.

For organizations looking to take training to the next level, visit us at www.cyberbossconsulting.com to learn more about The Lab or to inquire about utilizing our vetted instructors to provide hands-on training for your team members.

Cyber Boss Consulting ensures all instructors undergo industry-standard background checks, and we prioritize resilience and compliance in every engagement.

We are proud to maintain active contracts with healthcare organizations and government entities. References are available upon request at our discretion.

✨ Wishing you much success on your journey. To all of our readers and aspiring cybersecurity professionals, we are rooting for you as you break into and grow in this exciting field.

~The Cyber Boss Team

www.ingramcontent.com/pod-product-compliance
Lightning Source LLC
Chambersburg PA
CBHW071111210326
41519CB00020B/6263